Advance Payment

Nachoem M. Wijnberg

Advance Payment

Poems from
Songs, *The Life Of*
and *First This, Then That*

Translated and introduced
by David Colmer

ANVIL PRESS POETRY

Published in 2013
by Anvil Press Poetry Ltd
Neptune House 70 Royal Hill London SE10 8RF
www.anvilpresspoetry.com

This book is published with financial assistance
from Arts Council England
The publisher gratefully acknowledges the support
of the Dutch Foundation for Literature

Designed and set in Monotype Fournier by Anvil
Printed and bound in Great Britain
by Hobbs the Printers Ltd

ISBN 978 0 85646 450 8

A catalogue record for this book
is available from the British Library

CONTENTS

From *The Life Of*

From *Songs*

NACHOEM M. WIJNBERG (the M. is for Mesoelam) has published fourteen volumes of poetry and is generally seen as one of the most important and influential of modern Dutch poets. Although his early work evoked considerable resistance from confused and sometimes exasperated critics, Wijnberg stuck to his poetic guns and enjoyed a steady stream of praise as well. In recent years this has built up to a flood, with the three volumes represented in this collection, *First This, Then That* (2004), *Songs* (2006) and *The Life Of* (2008), winning, respectively, the Jan Campert Prize, the Ida Gerhardt Prize and the VSB Poetry Prize, the last mentioned being the Netherlands' most prestigious prize for a volume of poetry.

Wijnberg was born in Amsterdam in 1961 to parents who were products of the well-established Dutch Jewish community and able to trace their ancestry in the Netherlands back to the late seventeenth century. Although atheists, they raised him in a kosher household so that he would have a reasonable grasp of the Law and sent him to the Jewish secondary school in Amsterdam, where each day began with an hour of Talmud lessons. Wijnberg began his academic career by studying physics alongside law and economy. He eventually dropped the physics, but graduated in Law and Economics, going on to do a Ph.D. at the Rotterdam School of Management: first in economic law, but later changing his field of research to industrial economics and entrepreneurship. The title of his dissertation was *Innovation, Competition and Small Enterprises*.

After taking his Ph.D. Wijnberg taught and carried out research in a broad range of fields – from international trade to technology policy and from the history of technology to business ethics and strategic management – before becoming more interested in the cultural sector and focussing on the economic and managerial aspects of cultural industries. In 2005 he became the first professor of Cultural Entrepreneurship and Management at the University of Amsterdam Business School, a chair he holds to this day.

Besides his literary work, which includes four novels with a fifth forthcoming, Wijnberg has numerous academic publications to his name, with titles such as *The Dynamics of Inter-Firm Networks in the Course of the Industry Life Cycle: The Role of Appropriability* and *Groups, Experts and Innovation: The Selection System of Modern Visual Art.* (Both co-written.) Referring to his prolific poetic output, he has joked that it's a good thing he has to spend so much time on his university work as otherwise it would get completely out of hand. (A quip he may have come to regret, given its tendency to resurface in reviews every time he publishes a new volume of poetry.) In a more serious moment, he hinted at the entanglement of his academic and literary selves: 'A poem must say something that is correct, just as the assertions in an academic article must be correct. Similarly, those assertions mustn't be trivial; they have to appeal to the reader's emotions. I feel strongly about things like employment, banks and poverty, and expect other people to feel the same way.'

The drive and productivity of Wijnberg the poet leads to an output and success that can only do Wijnberg the business studies professor proud. A telling anecdote is the poet's account of how he began submitting poems to literary magazines as a university student and went at it with such verve and enthusiasm that he was eventually able to supplement his Ph.D. student's salary with a princely 1,000 guilders earned annually from the publication of poems in small magazines.

Wijnberg's poetic language is characterised by a combination of simplicity and abstraction. Almost anecdotal statements are rendered impersonal and abstract by the use of pronouns like 'someone', 'somebody', 'anyone' and 'anybody' and especially by an unspecified 'he' (= 'hij' in Dutch) that refers back to one of these 'someones' or 'anybodies' or to characters like 'a doctor'. This is normal and completely accepted usage in Dutch but poses a problem for the translator into English, where it's old-fashioned at best and sexist at worst. The bureaucratic 'he or she' is clearly impossible and a radical rephrasing to avoid Wijnberg's 'hes' would purge the poems of their characteristic self-reflexive entanglements. In the more classical poems, like the Chinese series, I have maintained 'he' as a traditional form, and in modern settings I have sometimes followed contemporary colloquial usage with a non-sexist 'they'. In other cases, though, it seemed as if Wijnberg was relating an anecdote about one specific person who remained unnamed but happened to be male: here too I followed his usage with 'he'.

With word choice in general, it was important to resist the temptation to get fancy or start dodging repetition; Wijnberg's vocabulary is stripped bare and elegant variation really is the last thing on his mind. In an interview in the Dutch daily, the *NRC*, he explained: 'I like to use simple words like table, chair and plant because their associations are general. A more specific word like cactus is burdened by a shedload of particular symbolism and associations. That can disrupt the rest of the poem. At the same time, I try to be as precise as possible. The more general I remain, the stronger the poem. The evocativeness of a poem increases as the number of things it can be about increase.'

The underlying grammar is usually relatively straightforward, but the use of nonspecific words and especially phrases sometimes creates eddies within the sentences that turn them into mental tongue-twisters. Wijnberg claims in that same *NRC* interview that his poems are 'clear' and 'easy to read' and 'at least promise to be about the important things in everyone's life.' This perspective may come as a surprise to some readers, but should perhaps be taken more as a recommendation of how to read the poems than a gibe at the critics who labelled him obscure and difficult at the start of his poetic career.

Wijnberg's erudition is obvious from the range of sources he draws on in his poetry, sources that are often explicitly acknowledged in the titles: Chinese and Urdu poets, Spinoza, Kepler and Rodin, the Bible, Jesus Christ and Zen Buddhism; the list goes on. He takes stories, lines and ideas from these sources and recasts them in his own style, combining them with abstracted anecdotes, thoughts, images and jokes to create unmistakable Wijnberg poems.

A relatively recent development has been the marked differentiation between volumes. Wijnberg: 'In my first volumes I used a range of forms. Later I got better at choosing and utilising forms. In my most recent volumes I have limited myself to one form for each volume, as a unifying factor. [With *The Life Of*] I reached a stage where I noticed that letting the sentences carry on made it possible for me to create different kinds of rhythms that brought out new tensions and added layers of meaning. And once you get the idea that a new form works, you dare to do more and more – even a timorous person like me.'

In an essay in the Dutch literary magazine *De Revisor*, Wijnberg's current editor, Bertram Mourits, attempts to explain the polarisation in the reception of Wijnberg's work by arguing that the negativity of some critics is at least partly due to preconceived notions of what poetry is and should be; what it can and must do. 'You have to unlearn how to read poetry before you can read the poetry of Nachoem M. Wijnberg.' According to Mourits, some critics are stymied by the bareness and lack of poetic devices – 'Serious poetry that can't be disentangled with the poetry reader's toolkit is problematic for a poetry reviewer' – but also because of their analytic compulsion. Of course, poetry like Wijnberg's that draws heavily on literary and historical sources throws down a gauntlet, but Mourits argues that complete identification and understanding of the references is not what these poems are about. 'It is interesting to know what he is using and what he does with it, but do you need to plunge into a library to understand a poem like "Su Dongpo"? Whether it's Cicero, Su Dongpo or King David: in the poems they speak Wijnberg's language. They are fashioned to the context in which they appear: Wijnberg's poems. The sources make the poetry as difficult as you want it to be.'

Mourits likens Wijnberg's poetry to philosophy, 'not airy-fairy philosophy in search of higher things, but analytical philosophy, in search of the meaning of the world and reality.' Poet and critic Hans Groenewegen has described his work as 'legendary anecdotes [...] attempts to use the techniques of legend to reveal the connections between things [...] giving the impression that a precise and unadorned account of particular events that take place in an apparently meaningless world can float unexpected meaning up to the surface.' The poet himself has explained the poems in *The Life Of* by saying that 'many of the poems have a surface layer with a narrative structure and in the ones that don't, there's a structure in the form of a line of reasoning. Of course, some connections are made by association (name a poem that doesn't do that), but in these poems those links are completely subordinate to the stories and reasoning. There's no "post-modern" cut and paste and alienation is the last thing I'm trying to achieve – the world is strange enough as it is and my poems aim to help in dealing with that strangeness by bringing it closer and, as far as that's possible, understanding it.'

While translating these poems, I worked in close consultation with the poet and I would like to thank him for the clarifications, explanations and advice that helped me to craft English versions that aim to have a similar effect in English as the original poems in Dutch. Hopefully this book can serve as an advance on the rapidly expanding oeuvre of this major European poet.

DAVID COLMER
Amsterdam, January 2012

From

First This, Then That

FIRST THIS, THEN THAT

Writing, then waiting;
    waiting, then writing;
a poem, then a goodbye,
    then visiting someone.

Longing, then choosing;
    exams, then waking with a start from exams;
visiting someone,
    then making him leave his house.

He's run away frightened,
    won't be coming back.
Waiting the night in his house,
    in the morning doing what I would otherwise forget.

A poem must be about something; otherwise no one can say
if the poem is superfluous if it is about him.

What he can say, what is in his heart: a poem if one is bigger
than the other,
disappointed if it is not a good poem.

Someone else can forget the words that are too big or too small
like balls he has thrown in the air quickly one after the other,

but take away his poems and what does he have left?
He wants to write more poems, enough to fill half the world.

Teika goes to visit his father, Shunzei, after Shunzei's wife,
    Teika's mother, has died.

Autumn has begun and a strong cold wind is blowing.
    Shunzei looks sad and lost.

After returning to his own house Teika writes that the wind
    longs for those who are no longer there.

Shunzei replies that autumn has begun, a cold wind is blowing,
    and he is still weeping with grief.

Shotetsu says that he doesn't need to explain why the poem
    Teika wrote is painful.

Because Shunzei is old and writing to his son, he doesn't want
    to say he can't go on,

that is why he says that it is autumn and the wind is cold.
    A difficult poem and a good one.

IF SOMEONE ASKED SHOTETSU THIS, THIS IS HOW HE WOULD ANSWER

In which province is Mount Yoshino;
    in which province, Mount Tatsuta?

When I write about cherry blossoms, Yoshino;
    when I write about autumn leaves, Tatsuta.

That doesn't help me to remember
    that one is in the province of Ise, the other in the
province of Hyuga.

But although I have never bothered to learn it by heart,
    I have discovered that Mount Yoshino is in the province
of Yamato.

If my house burns down with all my poems,
    I can get some back from those who have learnt them by
heart.

I won't dare to ask for the poems about who I desired.
    That's why I'll write them again when I remember who
I desired.

I'm going on a journey to write poems
and taking someone with me to help with what needs to be done
every day,

who can also write if someone we have spent the night with
asks for a poem:
he writes a poem and then we move on.

What I am capable of is not enough,
but today for the first time it was enough to show I had heard
the question.

He says that he is tired and going back without me.
Why not go on with me? Because this is the first question I
have asked him.

Don't misunderstand me, good night, left behind in the dark.
This was written by the one who came with me and helped
as if I had asked him to.

END OF THE VISIT

Walking with you part of the way,
able to say goodbye when you choose.

At most afraid that I will no longer want to see
what I saw with you when you came for a short visit.

Having to walk back by a different route, one I don't know;
I'll be surprised if I'm back in my house by dark.

At most afraid that one day I will no longer be able to bear
listening to music I know.

You don't need to wait, you leave and can say
when the goodbye is enough.

Tao Qian on Tao Qian:
He likes to read and is satisfied with the most simple of
explanations.
When he understands what something means, he is so happy he
forgets to eat.

Su Dongpo on Tao Qian:
He writes the way someone who is no longer impatient speaks.

Huang Tingjian on Tao Qian:
The poems are of no use
to someone just out of childhood,
but if he rereads them when he is old
it is as if he has made his decisions without knowing enough.

Huang Tingjian says that Su Dongpo is like Tao Qian.

Like two ducks, sleeping next to each other on the bank of the
river that carries the rain to the sea while the storm rages on.

SU DONGPO AND THE TRICK HE SAYS
HE LEARNT FROM TAO QIAN

The simplest way to find tranquillity:
keep starting over in a different way.

He knows nothing about those who find tranquillity,
free from what surrounds them; he's never met anyone like that.

Let's send him somewhere else, see if he changes his tune then.
His trick is to be more than happy when things are going well.

It's a warm evening and it will rain later.
More to see left and right than he can list.

Quiet, except for old man Du Fu reproaching old man Tao Qian
for being restless about what he doesn't have enough of.

Poems are useless for governing the world,
says Huang Tingjian, whose poems are miraculous when they
succeed.
If doing one thing is better than doing another, if they are both
done well,
is doing something like that one better than doing something
like that other?
Can't I say that in fewer words?
After all a poem shouldn't be wasteful.
But now I come to the more important problem:
settling for something that is like that better one because it is
like that better one?
Now and then I act as if I can do something well, says Su
Dongpo,
like something I need to start over again at once.

HAN YU AND MENG JIAO ARE FRIENDS; HAN YU ALSO BECOMES FRIENDS WITH JIA DAO, WHO TRIES TO WRITE LIKE MENG JIAO BEFORE SUCCEEDING IN DOING IT ANOTHER WAY

Meng Jiao is buried on a cold sunny day;
Jia Dao walks until he stops feeling sad.

Jia Dao thanks Han Yu for writing to him more than once
when Jia Dao was too ill to leave the house.

Jia Dao bumps into Han Yu when he's not watching where he's going
because he can't choose between two words.

At the end of each year Jia Dao puts that year's poems
in a pile and reads them one after the other.

I'm sitting next to Jesus in the ugliest church I've ever sat in
tired.
He points and asks, who's that? I say, that's you.
But I'm on a cross? You're on a cross.
What can I do about it? Ask the man who's sweeping the floor
without looking.

JOHN OF THE CROSS

What does the little monk do?
He draws a picture of Jesus on the cross
and nails the paper to a wooden cross.

What kind of work does the little monk get?
Doing what he can do quickly.

Sitting still is impossible
and meanwhile Jesus strips him of everything
he has from Jesus.

What does the little monk say when they play music for him?
Pay the musicians and thank them.

What is the little monk good at?
Giving up what he does

after Jesus has left him,
leaving him alone,
leaving him where no roads go.

JOHN OF THE CROSS

I am not honest
and I can't be where I want to be,

my departure unnoticed,
the house already asleep.

I heard someone singing
on the street: love leaves me
behind in the dark,
what should I do?

Stewed pears with cinammon
for the one who escaped in the dark,
hidden from view,

and when I come back
I'm not honest
and I haven't been there.

IN MY HOUSE ON THE WATER

I write poems,
    answer them,
I'm not scared
    that something is over,
just that it will make me less happy
when it comes back.

I thought: a storm,
    but there is no wind.
A big bright moon
    over the water.
If this is someone's dream,
    it will be broken and shared out.

Early in the morning
    the round moon
in the blue sky;
    I no longer ask
how I ended up here
or what they still owe me from before.

SONG

What happened to me is.
      Just don't ask.
The way you came in.
      Just don't ask.
I am still where you know I am.

You bring secrets
      like the mail that comes every day.
These words as good as any
      to deliver the latest news
about the things you know about.

From a house of loss to a house of loss.
Only you can ask if a different order is possible.

Just ask
your heart, ask yourself,
what you know of the blue
of the morning that departed from the night.

QUIET

Quiet, you say.
      I hardly hear you.
You're already that far.
      Don't leave me behind like this.

I stop talking.
      Immediately so dizzy
I have to hold myself tight.
      Quiet, you say.

I miss your laugh so much
      I imitate it,
louder and louder.
      That's as quiet as I can be.

Both shoes?
You take off a shoe
    when a woman comes to visit
and you don't want to marry her.

    First silence, then explanation;
first clear, then surprising;
    first the right shoe, then the left shoe,
then the left sock, then the right sock.

Is there anyone who wouldn't want to write a poem about that?
There is something else I mustn't forget to do, but I don't need
to think about it now.

Du Fu says of himself that he was a child prodigy, that he was
writing poetry when he was seven or eight years old. When
he's over forty, he will be a great poet. What he can think
about, he can write about.

A child asks if something is important enough to think about.
Is this an excuse to get out of doing something else?
The other children are already at work.
Reading takes time, just like looking round.
Every word Du Fu uses, he read somewhere.
He remembers the meaning of words the way he knows what
he's writing about.
The words themselves as if they are the words that belong to
what he's writing about.
In the order that someone would say them out loud
if they were given all the words of the poem in one go.

POEM FOR A FRIEND

I might just as well stop writing poetry;
no one else can tell me what the words mean.
It's been a long time since I dreamt of you; I've grown old.
I write this half joking, waiting for you, who won't write back
to make the joke whole; others send what they would have
thrown away otherwise
and don't write back when I answer.
Here are some tired words I mean
and words that have grown old in poems I try to understand.

MAN IN THE MOUNTAINS

A boy and a girl lean their bikes against a tree
and skate circles on the pond in front of the building.

All the floors are deserted because it's Sunday.
The lights in the corridors are dimmed.

Outside it's misty and it will get dark early.
I have a man in the mountains who works for me.

I don't know in advance how long I will manage
trying to work somewhere; that's why I have a man in the
mountains.

MAN IN THE MOUNTAINS

I feel happy, sad,
but happy and sad belong to a man in the mountains
and I only need to look out for him, that is what I want to
propose
to my man in the mountains.

I don't need to wait until I am old
to stop working in an office because I have a man in an office,
and I can feel happy or sad
because I have a man in the mountains.

Su Dongpo makes his own wine.
Whoever drinks that wine has heartburn for at least a week.

Su Dongpo makes his own ink from soot,
burning this, burning that, and almost burning down the house.

Su Dongpo makes his own medicine to live forever.
He's too excitable to live forever.

Try to think about a calm landscape in which he stands and
looks around.
That landscape might exist but trying won't help you get there.

Don't grow bitter about what has been taken away, but don't
forget it either.
What has been taken away deserves better.

From

The Life Of

As if he makes a decision every day that is as good as if he'd
been able to spend his whole life thinking about it.
The life of Kant, of Hegel, the days of the life of, choose three
or four.
Relate what he learnt in those days as if he was the last person
to know so little.
Give me something to cross off against then I can prepare
myself.
The reward is that I can go on with what I am doing, it doesn't
matter how long it takes.
This has nothing to do with everything staying as it is if I say
that I no longer want anything else.
I couldn't say anything in which one and the other occur in a
way that I, if I knew something to cross that one off against,
could no longer do it.
The stars above my head and being able to say what goes with
what if I've let them in.

I go to live in a village high in the mountains, the sea couldn't be further away.

I tell a girl, the daughter of the family I rent a room from, that she would do better to marry a postman or a lawyer.

She says she would rather have me and that I have to go live in another house or a hotel so that I can walk to her house on the morning of the wedding.

Boys and girls, I am new here, ask me if there's something I'm good at, it's easy to see what I'm not good at.

Ask if maybe I can keep doing the same thing all night without stopping, except to go and stand on the balcony for a moment.

Like a man whose turn it is to propose an answer and if he succeeds he can go someplace where he is all alone to watch the sun come up early in the morning, when else does the sun come up?

If it's another man's turn as well, they will go simultaneously to the same hotel in the mountains and see each other at breakfast and dinner.

If, in the night, one of them thinks of a reply to the other's last answer, he will tell him at breakfast.

If, in the night, he himself has thought of a new answer, he won't say what it is until dinner, skipping breakfast and going walking in the mountains.

Or else he will stay in his room and write a play about a boy in a village in the mountains who finds a proof for a mathematical theorem at the same time as other boys in other villages.

In every village there is at least one person whose behaviour is so predictable the other villagers can set their clocks when that person walks past.

Do you know how long she will be allowed stay with me, not long, I tie myself to her and they cut the rope.

This is how I am sent away from the house, they give me a stick to help me with walking because I have to walk until I can no longer see the house.

They don't give me any bread because I won't be able to eat it anyway, my eyes full of tears as I look at it.

Because I don't want to decide to use up the last of something.

It's not difficult to make me cry, that's nothing new to me.

IF I BORROW ENOUGH MONEY, THE BANK BECOMES MY SLAVE

A bank lends me money, if I don't pay it back they tell my boss
he has to pay my salary to them.
But they have to leave me enough to eat and sleep and an
umbrella when it's raining.
They can also empty my house, the furniture's not worth much
but every little helps.
Every morning I go to work, if I don't start early they will
soon find someone else and then no bank will lend me money
while the sun shines.
My boss has given me a cat to raise as a dog.
I know it's impossible, but I've asked for a whole week – maybe
the cat will get lucky, maybe I'll get lucky.
My hands around a cup of coffee before I go to work, warm-
empty, cold-empty, as if hidden in the mist over a lawn.
What I get if there's no work left for me, I'm ashamed to say
how little it is.
Once I'm outside I count it, if they look out through the
window they can watch me.
Imagine if it was so much that I had to count for hours, it gets
dark and I'm still standing there.
They stay on to watch a little longer after they've finished
work, but have to go home, I understand that, I could go home
too and carry on counting there.
If it's short, running back straightaway won't help because
they're all gone, and if I come back tomorrow I could have
spent what's missing that night.
Going somewhere where it's warm enough to walk around in
the daytime without any clothes on, it helps me to know that
something is more there than here.

For someone like me there's work everywhere, it shouldn't take more than a week to find a job for me.

Three jobs and three houses close to those jobs, I can choose one and try it for a week to see if I want to stay.

At the end of the week, if I don't want to stay, I come back immediately, then it was a week's holiday.

OVER THE WATER

We're in a boat, a storm comes up and you're asleep.
I wake you and say that I'm scared and you're asleep.
You ask the wind to quiet down and the water becomes still.
Afterwards you don't go back to sleep, you get out of the boat
and walk on over the water.
So far that I can hardly see you anymore and I call you and you
turn around and walk back to me, is that you?
I ask if I can walk beside you over the water.
I get out of the boat, start walking and sink into the water, but
your hand grabs mine and you pull me up so that I can get back
into the boat.
There may not be an explanation for everything that happens,
but you or I need to be able to explain everything I tell you.

I TRY TO TALK TO YOU AS IF I'M SAYING THIS FOR THE FIRST TIME AND THOUGHT OF IT WHEN I SAW YOU

I hope you don't mind my talking to you like this, if you'd known how I felt before I started, you would have walked off at once.
Oh, you want something for nothing, my apologies, I hadn't realised.
What wants to be remembered as it passed, a season says goodbye, that is the season in which something will be postponed until the end of the season.
When I was a child I played with trains and before going to bed I would take the most beautiful engine in my hand to look at closely one more time.
Later I became an engine driver, the train every day and the landscapes that came with it: sunsets, dawns, nights full of snow.

I've lost something that's not worth much, a cap I stuffed into
my coat pocket because it had stopped raining
I must have four or five of those caps, this one was old and I
could no longer wash the smell of rain out of it.
I'm good at that, if I go somewhere I leave half of what I've
brought with me lying around.
I'll never learn what to take with me if someone follows me to
give me what I left lying around.
That's how I know that something is too late, because I've
learnt something, no one could have explained it to me
beforehand.
You bring me the wallet I left on the table in a restaurant.
The next day my wallet gets stolen and the police say it was you.
How is that possible, yesterday you came to give me what I'd
left lying around, today you steal the very same thing.
Yesterday you had the day off, you say, today you're working,
you're a thief.
Where we can talk some more: in a room of a house that's not
yours or mine or in the shade of a tree at the end of a sunny day.
Sharing a shadow with someone, when something can become
like someone who has done that.
If something is being made it can't be destroyed until it's
finished, a thief only steals something that's finished.
Where's it got you, you say, having been changed from a thief
into someone who can ask questions and give answers?

Someone who lived in the same street had rooms full of books,
but wouldn't lend me a single one.
I could hardly make it back home for thinking about those
books.
The man was a bookseller, how could I have forgotten
something like that?
That night I dreamt that I had taken all of his books home with
me and was reading them one after the other in bed.
My parents thought that because I loved reading so much I
could grow up to be anything I wanted to be.
They sold something they didn't need to buy me a book.
Quickly I learnt its contents by heart so they could sell the
book and buy me another.
I think about that when I have so many books that I ask for
more time to read them all and to reread the books I read as a
child.
What I wanted to be when I grew up, I'm too embarrassed to
say, I thought that writing would be the smallest part of it.
How I've learnt to cope with still wanting something better –
give it to me as a problem someone else can't solve.
Now I ask no more than to be able to read all of the books that
are being written.

POOR MAN

I don't get any news except for hurried clouds in the twilight.
If you're poor you have to pay more for the same thing.
If you want me to misunderstand you, you'll have to try harder.
Because you don't give me what I need and hoped to get
from you.
If I did something else for you now, wouldn't you be getting
too much?
Two or three questions I hadn't expected and I'm lost.
Someone yells, the poor man's paying.
The poor man is over there at a table.
He's reading the book he left here last year.
Look, now he's frightened.

If I was a doctor I would write a note to another doctor: At
your request I have looked at the boy who gets so many
headaches.
If you ask me, it's just that he tries to stuff too much into his
brain – he says he's working ahead so that he won't have to do
it later.
He asks me to tell him what I'm looking at and why, so that if
he grows up to be a doctor he'll already know.
Is there anything he's worried about? That it's easier to decide
to do something if he's already worked ahead in it and that's
why too often he chooses to do the thing in which he's had the
most opportunity to work ahead.

The doctor himself is ill – he asks me to say something like
that, this time about someone who is waiting to get undressed.
That's the doctor who is starting to ask why I pretend, trying
to give me hope.
If I want, he can try to be there when I open my eyes and he
will wave to me.
I keep having to make him speak louder, does this mean I'm
going deaf?
Am I the kind of person who, when they are choosing who can
go on and who cannot, says that his back hurts when he picks
up something heavy, asking whether he should go and stand in
this line or that one?
But I am still known as someone who, when a cat has fallen
over, for example, immediately sees what's happening and
helps it back up onto its feet.
Can I say something like that, but now about a life after a life?
He means as if I've got two for the price of one and haven't
actually had to pay for the second.

What I remember: lying on my back and seeing a blue sky.
Then lying on a table and on a table across from me someone
else is having his leg amputated.
Later I see the leg, still in a shoe, standing up straight in a
corner of the room.
It's the wrong leg and, while I'm looking at it, the doctor
apologises.
He says he often confuses left and right, but he's too
embarrassed to ask someone else which is which.
It's not all bad, he thought he could always solve problems like
this, but now he knows not to count on it.
Do I think I have a supply of arms and legs, and a reserve
supply, hidden so far back that I have to think all day before
I remember where?

I talk to doctors who have won the lottery: immediately after
they have heard the news and then every two, three years.
The first time I ask them what they are planning to do with
the money, later I ask what they have done with it.
They are almost always willing to answer, even if they have
lost it all again, and the first time I talk to them I do not
contradict them if they think I work for the lottery.
There are only a few who have lost it all, most of them have
bought a new house and something else they had always
wanted and put the rest in the bank.
Of all the doctors I talk to, there is only one whose wife left
him after he had won.
It made him feel sick at heart for a few days, but once he had
also spent a week longing for a woman who was dead.
At the end of that week the longing diminished, but then he
realised that he had now really lost her.
Most contented are the ones who give some of it away each
year: to a local hospital, for instance, to buy a new bed.
If I could do something new this late in life I would study
medicine, because doctors try even harder for colleagues.
The sick doctors I talk to tell me that this is really true, and
that it's a shame that I am not in any way a colleague.
Not even if I have studied everything they have studied,
because if I had already done something else before, I could
be a doctor and do something else on the side, or I would
know what they know in a different way, because of studying
it so late.

AT THE DOCTOR'S

Tell it to your doctor, if he's an old man he'll roll around on
the floor at your feet laughing.
A squashed cat with outstretched legs, like it's been kicked to
the side of the road, where would you like me to lie down?
If he's old enough, he's heard it before, otherwise I'll go away
and come back when he's older.
I walk until I find a wall to climb over and end up in a garden.
It's not a big garden, a man standing in it wouldn't think he was
far away from everyone else, he can tell where he is from the
stars above his head.
The stars disappear one by one, as if only one can be left.
Something goes wrong and none are left.
Someone somewhere lies laughing on the ground.
You write on the palm of my hand what I need to say to spend
a day alone with you.

FOLLOWING MY HEART WITHOUT BREAKING THE RULES

Sticking to the rules without sticking to the rules by going
where the rules no longer apply.
I could stick to the rules there too by applying them to things
that, from a great distance, resemble what the rules are about.
But why would I do that, to avoid confusing someone who is
looking at me from a great distance?
Behind this morning the morning when the rules are all I have
is getting ready.

A sunny afternoon, we can go out, it won't be at anyone's
expense.
I show you a street I walked through as a child, there were no
trees then or they were very small.
When I was a child I made a fishing rod from a stick, a piece of
string and a bent nail.
I moved the stick through the water and a fish got caught on
the nail.
I ran home crying with the fish dangling from the rod in my
hand, the cleaning lady took it from me.
Later she told me she had put the fish back in the water.
We come back when it's almost dark and don't act surprised,
that would be a sham.

RULES

If that's against a rule, it's one I can't obey, or so briefly I can't remember it later.

Besides, the rules are only there to remind me what it takes for me to do what I do better.

As far as that's concerned, there's no difference between the rules I find in a book and the rules I think up early in the morning.

I know that because I've just now made a rule, nothing has to obey it yet.

IF I TALK LIKE THAT YOU'LL THINK I COME FROM GRANADA

I wouldn't want to stay here even if it was warm and the sun was shining, but then I could close my eyes and lie down on my back.
If you were with me I wouldn't ask you to fuck here in the street, because then I couldn't say there's no one here to help me.
If I can fuck here in the street, I can also stay as if it's Granada I love.
I wait for the train back to where I want to stay if I have to stay somewhere, I've already said yes, but when I'm back there I think I can say no again.

WHEN I SIT DOWN AT MY TABLE THEY BRING ME A CUP OF COFFEE AND A GLASS OF WATER

A hat on my head when I come in, I don't take it off when I sit down.
I hang my coat up on a hook on the wall, next to the photo of a man sitting at the table I always sit at.
The first time I came in I asked who he was and they said he was dead.
But he knew just how to move his mouth to get every word right.
You can't learn that without shadow and mastery in dark layers around your heart, and the outside layer is your coat.

AT SEA

What I see is the sea, I who am acting like I am a dog, no better
way of playing for laughs.
Who I take on a trip around the world, what I need to have
before I can think about what I cannot yet explain.
A dinner guest as long as we're at sea, someone I start talking
to after we haven't spoken to each other for days.
If you want to call me something, call me admiral of the ocean.
Surprise, surprise, I hear you say.
Two out of three's not bad.
I had wanted to spend this evening with you.
I have come up with something else, but I can't say what it
means.
What I have come up with is right every time I try it out, but I
can't say why.

At first, after he has told me a story about himself, I can't think
of anything to tell in return. I ask if I can use his story as if it's
about me, not when he is present, of course.
I stop telling the story when I have one of my own, after all,
when people get older they no longer have to tell the stories
they told as a child.
He offers to help me, I can start the next morning.
I go into his house, walk up to his bed and gently wake him.
I don't need to turn on a light, it's the end of summer.
I repeat after him, word for word, as fast as I can, sometimes I
guess a word before he says it.
Then he starts again, changing a word, sometimes a few words
in a row.
I keep following his lead and we continue like that all day until
I can tell the story myself or until he wants to go outside.
If I have trouble remembering words, he shows them to me on
paper, then puts the piece of paper away, then we do it again.
This goes on for two weeks and after two weeks he says that
he wants his mornings back.
If I don't understand part of a story I try other words instead
of the words I've heard.
I can't sleep until I can relate what I remember, as if I have to
make a decision when I have heard a story.
No reason to cry, I am the happiest man on earth and the only
one left.
I sent some of them to the west, some to the east, and not one
came back.
That's because the earth is flat and they've fallen off the edge.
Now they can no longer tell me they wouldn't marry me if I
was the last man.

STYLE

The late style, as if it no longer matters, I might just as well say
something to make it easier to be in the same room with me.
The penultimate style is that in which everyone and everything
has a share in what I can't do.
It is clear from my poems that I will keep writing poems until
the end, about how someone walks home without having
earned anything that day, determined to carry on.
Advice to a beginner: don't be afraid to write in a style that is
elegant and astonishing.

Seeing a different play every day, not when evening has come, but in the middle of the day.
What I saw this afternoon: a slave who heard that he was free and thought that the house he had worked in his whole life was now his.
Yesterday I saw how someone had been made a slave and a court ruled that it wasn't right, but in the meantime he had been sold on to someone else and that person didn't need to give him back his freedom.
Last night it scared me, tonight I could talk to someone without telling them about it.

An actor on another actor: he turned from left to right and
stopped, at the same time gesturing slightly with his hand.
Being an actor was unbearably lonely if no one noticed him
doing it, the chill from its beauty went right through me.
Someone who always comes in too early or too late comes in
like that, a bad actor can do it now and then, only a very good
actor can do it all the time.
They are acting and they go on for too long or stop suddenly
and you can see they're glad to be allowed to stop.

The chance of someone not coming back is the greatest when they haven't been here long, that's why everyone talks to them as little as possible until they have come back at least once.

If you have started to long for them and they don't come back, and that happens again and again, no one else will want to talk to you.

I find it difficult to say something general without also saying something about the sunlight when they wave me goodbye.

When someone has just arrived they have so many questions and when I don't hear anyone else answering I say something that seems general but is about what I once experienced myself.

As long as I stay here I can listen in case they call me back, the complete inverse of the game children play when they have a chair too few.

They count each other out loud, pointing with a finger, starting over and over again, always including themselves.

Looking at the moon and the stars around it, as if it's how to get rich quick.

Wanting to know how it ends, as if two children are playing, I walk away before their game is finished.

The things that make me suddenly feel like I'm back and nobody's left.

At your place it's like being in a hotel, why is it strange to want to live like that, it's what people pay for, isn't it?

If I want to hear another reason, if someone sleeps in hotels often, that's where they know where they are in the dark.

I can also act like you're a guest at my place, please, wait until someone comes to show you to a table, and I'm that someone, good morning, you're saying it's almost noon?

I look at my watch and you're right, it's half eight, you must have overslept after a wild night, what do you mean you're too old for that?

You woke up because you thought someone was knocking on the door to your room, but it was the door of the next room, that's how exciting your life is.

Has someone already brought you coffee or tea, otherwise I'll bring it at once, here is the pot, I'll pour one for you and after that you can pour your own.

When you go out later, don't hesitate to ask directions from someone who looks like me, when he tells me this evening that he was able to help someone like you cross the road he will want to hug me.

That's nothing to be sneezed at because he's twice my size and I am so tired by then, because in the mornings I work here and in the afternoons I'm an emissary from up in the sky.

I think that it can also be the other way round, that what reveals something can also conceal it, that's why I always want at least two tricks to do the same thing.

You say that it can also be the other way round, using what conceals to get a better view, but you're so much closer to reality than I am, you notice sooner when you say something that isn't so.

LET ME WIN THE LOTTERY AND I'LL GIVE TEN PERCENT TO THE POOR AND IF YOU DON'T BELIEVE ME, YOU CAN DEDUCT THAT TEN PERCENT RIGHT AWAY

If I was a man standing in the street as if he'd fallen down out of the sky, I'd go from door to door, and no, I'm not trying to sell something.

Dogs stop barking when they see me, I don't frighten them, sometimes I pat them on the head.

If people let me in, I keep my coat on, and if they ask what I'd like to drink, I say a glass of water because that's no trouble to anyone.

You wait until I come to visit again, you don't have anyone left who can talk you out of it.

Towards morning I walk past the garden, asking out loud if the person who lived there still lives there.

Surely you wouldn't stay in a house like this unless it was to wait for someone to come back.

If I'm standing inside at the window you come up next to me and we look at the garden.

I say you stand nice and straight, you say the slightest breeze could blow you over.

Please, I'm not very brave anymore, let me forget some of this.

I remember I came to you once when the night was already over.

I've travelled for weeks to get here and now I'm here, it's over in one night.

It was already over when I arrived, but I had to stay a night before I could go back.

How long before I can say that the rest is mine: if I stay away longer, if I've been back for a day?

If I don't have any money, I can't; if I do, I'm not allowed to
stay at an expensive hotel; when can I?
No, I'm not the last man on earth, just the only one who's still
going to die, everyone calls me boy.
I'm not a dog, but today I want to be like a big dog that's been
abandoned in a park.
I run through the water in a pond that is so shallow it looks like
I'm running over the water.

SOMEONE WHO WANTS TO BLOW HIS BRAINS OUT FOR LOVE TAKES IT SERIOUSLY AND THAT IS IMPORTANT

I don't think I can watch you if you, the actors, can't admit
it's funny.
Someone dies, but that's halfway, and someone at the end, but
he kept saying he wanted to die.
Not that everyone always gets what they ask for, but nothing
happens to anyone without their having asked for it at least
once.
Like in a play with too many roles when I read it, but it's easy
when staged.
It's even easier when all the roles are for one actor, in haste and
regret that he met her so very late at night.
Please don't cry about what you have to say, otherwise I'll give
you lines, you can write down one hundred times: this is so
important no one can ask for it.

Two narrow beds to choose between, a metre between them, I
can't get used to it in four weeks.
The bedroom is elongated, a desk with a desk lamp at the other
end.
In the bathroom there is a small, deep bath in which I can squat
with water up to my shoulders.
When I'm eating and before going to sleep, I read Murasaki on
Genji; in the bath, Wodehouse on Bertie Wooster.
The door is ajar, a stripe of moonlight on the floor, later he
comes in, I know of no other book in which a man is so
beautiful.

Gorgias arrives in Athens as an emissary from Leontini, a city
in Sicily asking for help.

This is the same Gorgias who teaches how to go from one
proposition to another and how this can be used to win a court
case.

The way Socrates does in an Aristophanes play, but it is
Gorgias, not Socrates, who is prepared to teach anyone who
will pay him how to go from one proposition to another.

One of the two generals Athens sends to Sicily is Laches, the
general Socrates asks what courage means.

Afterwards they send three generals who disagree about
everything: Lamachus, Nicias and Alcibiades.

First conquer Sicily, then Carthage, Italy and Spain; a good
plan, but you'd need to send different generals, not Lamachus,
Nicias and Alcibiades.

When Alcibiades was a young man, Socrates let him sit by his
side day and night; couldn't he have taught him how to be a
better general in the meantime?

That's not a problem for Socrates, but for Plato; Socrates
knows how to walk home after a lost battle.

Continuing with what I do, recognising what might be
important enough to justify putting everything I have into it –
both of those are brave, aren't they?

I can learn to do both, but it is difficult to learn to do the two
things at once, and getting better at one doesn't make it easier
to get better at the other afterwards.

If I can be brave in both ways like someone who goes from
play to play, his life a succession of short trips and staying
where he pays per day, can I also be brave like a general and
vice versa?

Your aunt's garden is larger than my uncle's hat, that is a
sentence from a book for learning languages, three or four at
once.
The children have to help carry the books and papers, how else
will they get from school to the house and back again?
That's why the children know the way from school to the
house better than your aunt who teaches them; in the middle of
the summer holidays they're out the front ringing the doorbell.
What's possible in a garden, one person walking away from
another and the other watching until the first is out of sight.
What the moon is for, standing on the moon in earthlight.
Here comes your aunt and walking next to her is my uncle,
whom I have never seen, who doesn't have a hat on his head in
any of the photos.
My uncle wanted to work the land as a farmer and went in
search of a place to learn how, your aunt wanted to give a party
in her garden come spring.

I run and with each step I get lighter, my feet hardly touching the ground anymore.

I start to fall, but that doesn't worry me.

I lie on the ground, people look at me and touch me, an hour later I open my eyes again.

I'm able to say my name and the name of someone who will let me sleep at their house tonight.

What I know for sure is that this is how I would have it if it were up to me.

This was more than a year ago, but this afternoon I run and feel it coming closer again.

It doesn't feel good yet, but I know that if it started to feel good I would no longer be able to decide.

I know that I am somewhere I am often, but I can't see anything that tells me exactly where it is.

I go from running to walking, staggering from left to right to avoid falling.

I sit down on the ground, my hands tremble and my face is covered with sweat.

I don't get that many chances, that doesn't mean that if I get a chance to say no I have to say no.

Like when I say that I don't want something anymore because I can't stand thinking that it's the last time.

WHAT THE MAID TOLD MY MOTHER ABOUT
MY GRANDFATHER

My grandfather lived in a house with his mother, two sisters
and a brother, in a village of Christians.
The maid and the servants were born in the village, for his
sisters, he found two men to marry who had never visited the
village before.
He didn't think any woman was good enough for his brother,
who he also worked with, buying and selling sheep and cattle.
He couldn't take it anymore, said the maid, in the period
between the death of his mother and his own marriage.
He stayed inside for days on end and didn't speak to anyone,
he wanted to become a Christian, but didn't do it.

My grandfather is in his garden when the Christian comes to visit.

He can see how well his neighbours who believe in Jesus Christ are doing.

My grandfather says that he is doing well too.

That's an advance payment, the Christian says, because Jesus Christ assumes that later a man like my grandfather will start believing in him.

If he believed in Jesus Christ he would do better than his neighbours, because he is a better man and works harder.

He is sure of it, the Christian says, and could my grandfather cut down the biggest tree in his garden, as an advance payment?

My grandfather asks why, he doesn't believe in the tree, or do his neighbours think he does?

The Christian says that the neighbours don't think that my grandfather believes in the tree, just that the tree helps him.

They are stupid people, the Christian says, if Jesus Christ didn't take pity on them, they would be on the street and starving.

My father wrote letters to his brother and asked if I wanted to
read them, I said I preferred not to and I still wouldn't want to
now.

I know nothing about his brother except what my father told
me about him, a couple of photos and the last letters he wrote.
Someone from the railways made sure the letters got to my
grandparents and my father.

He wrote that he had heard that Uncle Lion was still alive,
surely he'd be able to manage too.

That was the only name he dared mention, he didn't sign as
Salmon but as Juda.

He called my father – who was fourteen at the time, his brother
twenty-three – dear boy, you know who I mean.

If my father arrived in New York without a cent, he'd drive
taxis because he was good at finding his way, even in cities he'd
never been to before.

There too he could have written letters to his brother, if his
brother hadn't followed him in time.

MY FATHER SAYS THAT IT IS SENSIBLE TO GET INTO SOMETHING IN WHICH MEDIOCRITY IS NO DISASTER, LIKE THE FIELD IN WHICH I AM A PROFESSOR

He decides to obey the law, as someone who doesn't know the law, but expects his children to know it, and therefore does what he can to avoid embarrassing them.

My father says that he became a mediocre man especially for me, so that no one would think I could never be as good as my father.

He would still like someone to remember him when he is no longer here, not every day, but now and then, without having planned it.

If what is left after someone's death is their part of truth, what happens to my part of untruth?

When someone is dead there is nothing left, except of my father, who walks around by himself where he is.

My father goes to America, my mother will die young, it could hardly be any other way with the work she does.

She cleans other people's houses and at the end of the day she gets a bowl of soup to take home with her.

At school I don't need to write anything down, I hear it once and then I know it forever.

If I do write something down, it's a poem, I enter the house and can't find my mother.

That's what makes me feel cold, as if I see her standing there and take a step towards her.

My father doesn't go to America, but we don't hear from him anymore.

Worried that a poem's not finished yet? I can write a poem whenever I like.

MAKE A WISH

I go to work, but remain silent until someone says something
to me.
I say I'm quitting, but a day later I ask for my job back.
Maybe I'll never find another job.
Wasn't that my dream, to swim with a cat?
What do I want to be, a Gypsy, who lives where there are no
more houses?
Are there any Gypsies left, I can't remember ever having seen one.
I point birds in the right direction and say, it's getting colder,
you'd better head south.
I know they don't understand the words, but they see me
standing there, pointing with out-stretched arm.
After the first snow has fallen, they see me standing in the snow,
that makes it even clearer.
I'm still here, not divided into two halves that someone could
walk between, I must have wished for something else.

A child comes up to me and says he wants to give away half
of what he has.
If he's done that, doesn't he have just as much reason to divide
what he has left once again into two halves.
He doesn't think so, because then he couldn't do anything else,
because there would always be something left to divide into
two halves.
If he divides, the other gets to choose, that's the rule to make
sure the two halves are fair.
Why to me? I thought the idea was to give something away to
those who are poorer than he is.
Instead of someone who's poorer, it can also be someone who's
more than twice as old, because how much something is worth
also depends on how much longer someone will have it.
Nearby there's a river I want to walk on, heading downstream,
and to my left and to my right it's growing dark.

WHAT I AM AFRAID OF AND WHAT I WOULD LIKE TO HAVE

I say what I am doing out loud, no need to wait for other
people to stop talking.
I keep my face still after I've said something, like an actor who
is not yet good at what he does but is allowed to join in because
of his looks.
I fall out of a high window or I go to live in another country,
like an actor who has been fired but can join in one last time.
I can be mistaken, I don't need to know everything, not even
everything I could have known beforehand.
I don't get enough time for that and I don't get any extra if
someone imitates me.
Sometimes I can guess beforehand how much time it will take
to find out something.
The only thing it takes is time, sometimes I know something
quickly.
If I could clap my hands and be somewhere I wanted to see
once again, would I also want to remember it at the same time?
Whatever the wind blows in, I take a step aside to let it through.
I admit that my two strongest longings are contradictory.
What I don't need to be afraid of: someone else taking away
something I want.
I can choose, the others will take what I leave, they've said so.
I have been rich, I don't need to be rich again, I've eaten, I
don't need to eat anymore, I've kept my eyes on someone
everyone looked at.
I say that I've decided not to do what I wanted to do, simply
because I can't do it well.
It's been done before, as well as possible, and when I was a
child I copied the way it was done, to better understand it.

If they tell me that I had better open my eyes quickly if I want to open them at all, will I want someone else with me when I do so?

When the actor who plays my life got his lines he didn't say that they were for a child.

I am talking about my life as if the person I am speaking to is new here, they haven't seen it yet.

I ask the actor to do it again, even though I know that he won't do it as well a second time.

If he doesn't remember some of it that well, but knows how it goes later, he will try to get there as fast as possible.

I'm not here to live, but to say goodbye to a few friends.

If you want to help me, suggest possibilities, even highly
unlikely ones, so that I don't overlook something.
Someone needs a new heart, but there aren't enough to go
round and there are others who can live longer with a new
heart.
If he is rich he can buy a new house but not a new heart, not
here at least.
Of course he could travel somewhere where it is possible, but
he is no longer able to travel – ha-ha!
I'm glad that I don't have to go on a trip tomorrow, but I don't
need to think about what I wanted to decide these last few days.
If I am in pain I cannot decide as well, I'm not in pain yet, what
can I decide today?
If it's a present, like a bunch of flowers a father gives his son
for his birthday, saying so as he does it.
The son is sitting in the back of the car next to the pump in a
petrol station, the father has gone in to pay and has bought the
flowers inside.
And something for himself too? If it's his son's birthday, then
it's kind of his birthday too, isn't it?
No, it's not his birthday at all. I'm too old for that on a day
that's my birthday.
Something I absolutely do not want is to suddenly be given
something and have to decide whether I want to keep it.
If I am told one morning that I have overlooked something,
and that really is the case, for a moment I can't speak.
Maybe someone is lying in bed with a heart that no one else
wants and that someone has almost stopped breathing – did I
say breathing, I meant reading.

Someone gives me what I asked for on my birthday, but if
someone asks what I want I can only say something easy.
I don't want to make a puzzle of it, knowing beforehand that I
have all the pieces, except when I've lost one during an earlier
attempt and get up in the middle of the night to search the
house.
You almost never propose anything that's any use to me, but
one morning you say something and I try to understand how I
could have overlooked it.
If someone can no longer speak, how much do I then say, that's
not something I can decide.

From

Songs

SONG

The last time I spoke to you,
I hardly got a word in,
the last time I spoke,
make that into a song.

I said I couldn't sing,
can you sing, I asked,
the last time I spoke to you,
I've never heard you sing.

SONG

In the light I don't get
what I wanted in the dark,
in the dark I don't get
what I wanted in the light.

On this side
the sun shines and on that side,
if I looked on that side,
there are clouds.

I no longer know
where left is, where right,
where reading, where writing,
but I can tell you what I hear.

As if written
by someone who can't write,
but says the words one by one
to someone far away.

HORACE SONG

At my age, boy or girl,
it's all the same,
the problem is
that nothing is better

than asking love
from who offers it
or am I being wise again
at someone else's expense,

like when I say that love
for me is also work?
When you loved me
and no one else

could touch your soft throat,
your flowing hair,
I loved more
than the king of Persia.

HORACE SONG

I thank the inventor
of the journey, also
inventor of the poem,
and guide to where

someone else has been for a long time.
Here's another one!
To the inventor of the poem I say,
let me be satisfied with what is

and keep writing as I grow old,
that is what I ask,
and for someone who knows
what it was like before,

if only yesterday,
it has grown dark, this year
will end like all the others,
if I celebrate New Year's tonight.

I KNOW

You want to go away.
Because they kill all the rabbits here.
But you're not a rabbit.
Try explaining that to them.

It's the rabbits that make it impossible.
No, it's you.
Why me?
Why the rabbits?

If charged by a savage rabbit,
act like you're dead.
I know that, you know that,
but does the rabbit know it?

And then the sun stops shining.
After how long?
After four days.
Thank you, I thought for a moment you said three days.

Was that it or did it get dark?
What did you think I wanted?
The same story over and over.
I wouldn't exchange you for anyone else.

SONG

I saw a shop
went in and bought
something I had forgotten
I already had.

I stood in the shop
and there was nothing else
I could remember
that I needed.

But what do I do
with two of them,
except wait
for one to break?

My father wanted
to teach me about money,
that's why he refused
to give me something.

He gave me money
and pointed to a shop,
go in and ask
for what you want.

IT IS FUNNY SONG

He says something and
everyone who hears
knows it's not true,
except the one he's saying it to.

He wants to tell a joke
over again, to get it right
this time, overcome
by what saddens.

Isn't it funny
that you talk about something
without mentioning
what it can't do without.

There's a joke that I
am allowed to tell once
a day, I thought once
a year, that's how it feels.

What has to be said
or left out gets guessed,
the memory
that calms the heart.

SONG

Touch it,
make it gold,
what skin is like
if it's gold
and still feels like skin.

What I do
when I see you,
I reach out to you,
stroke your face,
the eyes you close.

SONG

Not long ago
it rained hard,
not long ago
it got dark.

I didn't go on
until it had stopped,
so I had to wait
until it stopped.

I heard the rain
fall from great heights
and could have sat
outside on the grass.

The rain as a crown
on my head, or
as if I hadn't yet begun
and got to say when.

Like in a song:
once and once again,
afraid it has changed
or remained unchanged.

PARIS SONG

It is cold and old
as a park in Paris,
the capital of France.

I want to lie in bed
with someone who can spend a long time
thinking about one thing.

What is almost there,
the moon over a field,
a song far away.

The opposite of
what takes back promises
that haven't been made.

What I ask for,
letting what is too much be
as if it's almost there.

SONG

Now and then silence
without being sure
if the song goes on,
not daring to say
what I actually want.

I touch you
while listening,
if you weren't here
I couldn't listen
to a song like this.

SONG

I read life after life
and when someone's as old as I am
I hold my breath,
sometimes I look up when that was.

When I was younger
I sometimes skipped
where someone was a child,
I don't know why.

What I want to have with me:
a book that has enough to read in it;
when I'm old I won't give it away,
I'll sell it.

I also skip
when I get scared
that someone won't change anymore,
I only read how it ends.

What I want changes
from moment to moment,
even when I've had enough
I'm sad it's over.

MICHELANGELO SONG

Michelangelo says:
to make a thing that is like forgiveness
takes great effort and risk
of losing what one does not have.

Sensing a mistake before it happens,
but not knowing when and how large,
oh, and I forgot to say,
this is not actually what I wanted.

Michelangelo says, draw something every day,
draw something you see.
I must draw something today,
something I see.

Oh, I forgot to say,
this is not a dream,
I forgive you many things because of something
you said and have now forgotten.

You can feel love
for the first thing you see,
as long as you remember:
conclusion, balance, measure.

SONG

The way I lay in bed
after waking up first.
Why can I only remember
what I saw or thought
from when I got up, carefully?

What I listen to
because you listened to it,
and me without telling you,
waiting for you to come back,
alone in your house.

I want to go back there
without you,
that's not difficult,
you're nowhere to be found,
who'll stop me?

I try to think of
all possible disturbances,
enlarging them one by one
until I can measure them,
that's how one does an experiment.

Then I know what I have,
what I miss is,
why I feel the way I feel,
listening to
what has been listened to.

SONG

How I can show
that I've remembered
what you're like, just see
me imitate you.

No one who sees me
thinks I'm you,
but I am thinking of you
and nothing else.

STARTING SONG

It doesn't go the way I want it to:
I have to get in line
and when I get to the front,
the line is gone.

Today is the day
I can do what I like,
it is evening
and I don't know when the day began.

This evening I'll see you again,
you were away for a day,
you didn't know
what kind of day today is for me.

One or two days a year
of speaking quietly
with the lights on,
not days, they were evenings.

They're what I want,
not just evenings but also days,
days lined up,
and me at the front.

SONG

What is the difference?
An empty evening when
the one you didn't want to see
didn't even come,
and you had dressed for company.

If you go out
you can't be like a child
that's allowed to be alone
as long as it likes,
walking in the dark.

Stop me
if you've heard this one,
stop me, say,
what is the difference,
and make me still.

SONG

One night
I heard my father, my mother,
and my mother said
I should stop
playing music.

My father said,
let the boy
play his music,
when he no longer wants to
he'll still have all the time he wants.

When he realises
how little he needs,
in the morning or evening,
when he wants to do something
as heavy as what's no longer possible.

When he has just started
to play his music,
my mother said,
in the morning or evening,
when it's early or late.

I wanted to have
my father, my mother,
back again,
I wanted to give back
what I'd got from them.

MORNING AND EVENING SONG

It is silent above my head,
below my feet,
the dark's not cold, the light's not warm;
when morning or evening comes running up,
it's to bring me something to read.

A book I want to keep
or take with me when I travel;
on the first page
I stopped reading three times
and each time I could have stopped longer.

I suddenly dare to say
I want you;
if you've suddenly had enough
I have to accept it,
like when morning or evening has had enough.

What you gave me
is that I don't start today
with what was taken from me
or abandoned by me,
now spread out over mornings and evenings.

When I was a child
I lived in a house
I still have the key to
because I was given it to hold
the morning we left to travel until it was evening.

SONG

The night full of lights that say where, where not.

This is to sing, that's why there's repetition.

I have as long as it takes.

Good for a song because it takes so long.

I can't quite sing that song.

That's not true; I can't sing it.

Even if I don't find my heart where it was.

Don't change for me.

A NIGHT IN PARIS MAKES UP FOR EVERYTHING

It is late but starts anyway.

Play me the music that someone can dance that to, someone who can't sing.

If you play that music everyone will dance and ask for more.

And what of it? Just that!

Where have you been?

No, you've never been there.

Half an hour? An hour?

Like someone who's come with someone who's come for a short visit?

It's raining like I can't remember it ever having rained before.

If one of us no longer wants this, I'll go to Paris.

In Paris, on a day it's raining.

Does he know how it works? He invented it.

In Paris, from victory to victory, look, that man there is crowning himself.

The children in Paris are exceptionally gifted, three or four years old and they speak French fluently.